Chocolate Truffle Cookbook

Indulge in Decadent Chocolate Truffle Creations

CHOCOLATE TRUFFLE COOKBOOK

First edition. November 19, 2023.

ISBN: 979-8223912804

Written by Sammy Andrews.

Sammy Andrews

Chapter Outline:

Introduction to Chocolate Truffles

- The History of Chocolate Truffles
- Why Make Truffles at Home
- Getting Started with Truffle Making

Essential Tools and Ingredients

- Quality Chocolate Selection
- Essential Kitchen Equipment
- Other Key Ingredients

Classic Dark Chocolate Truffles

- Recipe: Basic Dark Chocolate Truffles
- Variations and Flavor Enhancements
- Rolling and Coating Techniques

Milk Chocolate Delights

- Recipe: Creamy Milk Chocolate Truffles
- Customizing Milk Chocolate Truffles
- Decorative Ideas

White Chocolate Elegance

- Recipe: Silky White Chocolate Truffles
- Flavoring White Chocolate Truffles
- Creative Decorations

Vegan and Dairy-Free Variations

- Recipe: Vegan Chocolate Truffles

- Dairy-Free Chocolate Options
- Vegan Coating and Decorations

Nutty Infusions: Almond, Hazelnut, and More

- Recipe: Nutty Chocolate Truffles
- Exploring Nut Flavors
- Nut Coatings and Garnishes

Fruity Flavors: Raspberry, Orange, and Beyond

- Recipe: Fruity Chocolate Truffles
- Fresh and Dried Fruit Infusions
- Fruit-Infused Coating Ideas

Boozy Truffle Treats

- Recipe: Boozy Chocolate Truffles
- Selecting and Using Liquors
- Alcohol-Free Alternatives

Coffee and Mocha Infused Truffles

- Recipe: Coffee Lover's Truffles
- Espresso and Coffee Flavoring
- Mocha Swirl Truffle Ideas

Spices and Herbs: Unique Flavor Combinations

- Recipe: Spiced Chocolate Truffles
- Spice and Herb Pairings
- Aromatic Spice Coatings

Healthier Options: Avocado and Coconut Truffles

- Recipe: Guilt-Free Chocolate Truffles
- Using Avocado for Creaminess
- Coconut and Healthy Sweeteners

Kid-Friendly Truffle Creations

- Recipe: Fun and Colorful Truffles
- Kid-Approved Flavors
- Kid-Friendly Decorations

Truffle Shapes and Decorations

- Shaping Techniques
- Decorating with Chocolate and Edible Elements
- Tips for Professional-Looking Truffles

Truffle Coating Techniques

- Mastering the Art of Coating
- Different Coating Options
- Troubleshooting Coating Issues

Tips for Perfectly Tempered Chocolate

- Understanding Chocolate Tempering
- Various Tempering Methods
- Troubleshooting Tempering Problems

Storing and Gifting Your Truffles

- Proper Storage Practices
- Gift Packaging and Presentation

- Homemade Truffle Gift Ideas

Truffle Troubleshooting

- Common Truffle-Making Challenges
- Solutions and Fixes
- Expert Tips for Success

Chocolate Pairings and Tasting Notes

- Chocolate Tasting Experience
- Flavor Profiles and Descriptions

Beyond Truffles: Desserts and Treats

- Using Truffles in Other Desserts
- Truffle-Inspired Dessert Recipes
- Creative Ways to Enjoy Chocolate Truffles

Chapter 1: Introduction to Chocolate Truffles

Chocolate truffles, those bite-sized morsels of pure indulgence, have a rich and fascinating history. They are the epitome of luxury and sophistication when it comes to chocolate treats. In this chapter, we'll delve into the origins of chocolate truffles, discuss why making them at home is such a delightful endeavor, and provide an overview of what you can expect in this delectable journey.

The History of Chocolate Truffles

The story of chocolate truffles is shrouded in legend and mystery. It's widely believed that these confections were named after the highly-prized underground fungi called truffles, due to their visual resemblance. The credit for inventing the first chocolate truffle is often attributed to Auguste Escoffier, the renowned French chef, in the late 19th century. However, the exact origins remain a topic of debate among culinary historians.

Chocolate truffles gained fame in France and quickly became associated with opulence and elegance. Their smooth, ganache-like centers and exquisite coatings made them a favorite among royalty and high society. Over time, these delightful creations spread beyond France's borders, captivating the hearts and taste buds of people around the world.

Why Make Truffles at Home

Making chocolate truffles at home is a gratifying experience that offers several advantages:

Quality Control: When you make truffles from scratch, you have complete control over the ingredients. You can choose the finest chocolates, customize flavors, and adjust sweetness levels to your liking.

Endless Creativity: Homemade truffles allow you to explore a wide range of flavors, from classic to unconventional. You can infuse them with your favorite ingredients, creating unique and personalized treats.

Gifts from the Heart: Handcrafted truffles make thoughtful gifts for friends and loved ones. Their artisanal quality adds a personal touch to any occasion.

Cost-Effective: While high-quality chocolates can be expensive, making truffles at home is often more cost-effective than purchasing premium truffles from a store.

Fun and Rewarding: Crafting truffles is a delightful culinary adventure. It's a creative process that can be shared with friends and family, making it an enjoyable and rewarding hobby.

Getting Started with Truffle Making

Before you embark on your chocolate truffle-making journey, there are a few key things to keep in mind:

Ingredients: Select the best-quality chocolate and other ingredients you can find. High cocoa content chocolate (around 70% cocoa) is typically preferred for truffle centers, as it offers a rich and intense chocolate flavor.

Equipment: You'll need basic kitchen tools such as mixing bowls, a saucepan, and a whisk, as well as optional items like truffle molds and a thermometer for tempering chocolate.

Technique: Truffle making involves a few fundamental techniques, including ganache preparation, shaping, and coating. Each step contributes to the final texture and appearance of your truffles.

Creativity: Don't be afraid to experiment with flavors and decorations. The world of chocolate truffles is as vast as your imagination, and you'll discover that even small variations can lead to wonderfully unique results.

In the chapters ahead, we'll explore a wide array of chocolate truffle recipes, from the classic dark chocolate truffle to exotic flavor combinations, allowing you to create a truffle collection that suits your taste and occasion.

Now that you've been introduced to the world of chocolate truffles, it's time to gather your ingredients and tools and prepare for a delicious adventure. In the following chapters, we'll dive deeper into the art of truffle making, starting with the timeless Classic Dark Chocolate Truffles in Chapter 3. Get ready to indulge in the decadent world of chocolate truffles!

Chapter 2: Essential Tools and Ingredients

In the world of chocolate truffle making, success begins with selecting the finest ingredients and having the right tools at your disposal. This chapter is your guide to making sure you're well-equipped to embark on your truffle-making journey.

Quality Chocolate Selection

The quality of chocolate you choose for your truffles plays a pivotal role in their taste and texture. Here are some key considerations when selecting chocolate:

Cocoa Content: Look for high-quality chocolate with a cocoa content of around 70%. This percentage indicates the amount of cocoa solids and cocoa butter in the chocolate. Higher cocoa content results in a more intense and robust chocolate flavor.

Chocolate Type: Choose between dark, milk, or white chocolate, depending on your preference and the flavor profile you want to create. Each type offers a unique taste experience.

Brands: Experiment with different chocolate brands to find your favorite. High-end brands often use premium cocoa beans and have a smoother texture.

Cocoa Origin: Some chocolates specify the origin of the cocoa beans, such as single-origin chocolates. These can have distinct flavor notes based on where the cocoa was grown.

Couverture Chocolate: Couverture chocolate is a high-quality chocolate that contains a higher percentage of cocoa butter. It's excellent for coating truffles due to its glossy finish and smooth texture.

Essential Kitchen Equipment

Now, let's talk about the essential tools you'll need to create perfect truffles:

Mixing Bowls: Choose heatproof mixing bowls in various sizes. These will be used for melting chocolate and preparing ganache.

Saucepan: You'll need a heavy-bottomed saucepan for melting chocolate and heating cream.

Whisk: A whisk is essential for mixing and emulsifying the ganache.

Spatula: A rubber spatula helps to scrape down the sides of bowls and saucepans, ensuring you use all of your ingredients efficiently.

Double Boiler or Microwave: A double boiler provides gentle, indirect heat for melting chocolate. Alternatively, you can use a microwave for short bursts of heat, stirring in between, until the chocolate is melted and smooth.

Thermometer: While not always necessary, a kitchen thermometer can be helpful for precise temperature control when tempering chocolate.

Piping Bag and Tips: These are useful for shaping truffles, especially if you want consistent sizes and shapes.

Truffle Molds: Truffle molds come in various shapes and sizes and can make the shaping process easier. They're not required, but they add a professional touch to your truffles.

Wax Paper or Parchment Paper: This is used for lining trays and shaping truffles.

Other Key Ingredients

Aside from chocolate, there are a few key ingredients that are essential for making truffles:

Heavy Cream: Use high-fat heavy cream to create the creamy ganache centers of your truffles. The fat content is crucial for achieving a silky texture.

Flavoring Agents: Depending on your truffle recipe, you may need extracts (e.g., vanilla, almond), liqueurs, fruit purees, or spices to infuse flavors into your ganache.

Butter: Some truffle recipes include butter, which adds richness and creaminess to the ganache.

Coatings: Consider a variety of coatings such as cocoa powder, powdered sugar, chopped nuts, coconut flakes, or colored sprinkles to coat your truffles and add texture.

Now that you have a solid understanding of the essential tools and ingredients, you're ready to embark on your chocolate truffle-making adventure. In the following chapters, we'll start creating truffles that will leave you and your loved ones craving for more. Next up is Chapter 3, where we dive into the world of Classic Dark Chocolate Truffles, a timeless favorite among chocolate enthusiasts. Get ready to melt, mix, and mold your way to truffle perfection!

Chapter 3: Classic Dark Chocolate Truffles

Dark chocolate truffles are the epitome of chocolate luxury. With their intense cocoa flavor and velvety ganache centers, they're a timeless favorite among chocolate enthusiasts. In this chapter, we'll guide you through crafting the perfect dark chocolate truffles and explore variations that will elevate this classic treat to new heights.

Recipe: Basic Dark Chocolate Truffles
Ingredients:

- 8 ounces (227 grams) high-quality dark chocolate (around 70% cocoa), finely chopped
- 1/2 cup (120 ml) heavy cream
- 2 tablespoons unsalted butter, softened
- 1 teaspoon pure vanilla extract (optional)
- Pinch of salt
- Coating of your choice (cocoa powder, powdered sugar, or chopped nuts)

Instructions:

1. Prepare the Chocolate: Place the finely chopped dark chocolate in a heatproof bowl.
2. Heat the Cream: In a saucepan over medium heat, warm the heavy cream until it begins to simmer. Remove it from the heat immediately; do not let it boil.
3. Create the Ganache: Pour the hot cream over the chopped chocolate. Let it sit for a minute to melt the chocolate. Add a pinch of salt and vanilla extract if desired. Gently stir until the mixture becomes smooth and glossy.
4. Incorporate Butter: Add the softened butter and stir until fully

incorporated. The ganache should be creamy and shiny.

5. Chill the Ganache: Cover the bowl with plastic wrap, making sure it touches the surface of the ganache to prevent a skin from forming. Refrigerate the ganache for at least 2 hours, or until it becomes firm enough to handle.

6. Shape the Truffles: Once the ganache is chilled, use a spoon or a melon baller to scoop out small portions. Roll them into bite-sized balls and place them on a tray lined with wax paper.

7. Coating: Roll the truffles in your preferred coating. You can use cocoa powder for a classic finish, powdered sugar for a sweet touch, or chopped nuts for a delightful crunch. Ensure the truffles are evenly coated.

8. Chill Again: Return the truffles to the refrigerator for about 30 minutes to set.

9. Serve and Enjoy: Your classic dark chocolate truffles are now ready to be savored. Store them in an airtight container in the refrigerator for up to two weeks, although they are unlikely to last that long!

Variations and Flavor Enhancements

While classic dark chocolate truffles are exquisite on their own, you can elevate them with creative variations and flavor enhancements:

Fruit-Infused: Add a burst of fruity flavor by incorporating fruit purees like raspberry, orange, or passion fruit into the ganache.

Spiced Delights: Experiment with spices like cinnamon, cardamom, or chili powder to give your truffles a warm and exotic twist.

Liqueur-Infused: A splash of your favorite liqueur, such as Grand Marnier, Amaretto, or Irish cream, can infuse your truffles with sophisticated adult flavors.

Nutty Crunch: Mix finely chopped nuts (such as almonds, hazelnuts, or pistachios) into the ganache or use them as a coating for added texture and flavor.

Rolling and Coating Techniques

Achieving perfectly round and evenly coated truffles takes practice. Here are some tips for mastering these techniques:

Hand Rolling: Use your hands to roll ganache portions into balls. Keep your hands lightly buttered or dusted with cocoa powder to prevent sticking.

Uniform Sizing: For consistent truffle sizes, consider using a small cookie scoop or a melon baller.

Coating: When coating truffles, it's essential to work quickly while the ganache is still firm. Place your coating of choice in a shallow dish, and gently roll the truffle to cover it evenly.

Shaping Tools: If you prefer uniformity, invest in truffle molds that can help you create perfectly shaped truffles with ease.

Now that you've mastered the art of crafting classic dark chocolate truffles, you're well on your way to becoming a truffle-making maestro.

Chapter 4: Milk Chocolate Delights

Milk chocolate truffles offer a creamy and slightly sweeter alternative to their dark chocolate counterparts. In this chapter, we'll guide you through the process of creating silky and indulgent milk chocolate truffles, explore ways to customize them, and provide decorative ideas to make your creations even more delightful.

Recipe: Creamy Milk Chocolate Truffles

Ingredients:

- 8 ounces (227 grams) high-quality milk chocolate, finely chopped
- 1/2 cup (120 ml) heavy cream
- 2 tablespoons unsalted butter, softened
- 1/2 teaspoon pure vanilla extract
- Pinch of salt
- Coating of your choice (cocoa powder, powdered sugar, or colored sprinkles)

Instructions:

1. Prepare the Chocolate: Place the finely chopped milk chocolate in a heatproof bowl.
2. Heat the Cream: In a saucepan over medium heat, warm the heavy cream until it begins to simmer. Remove it from the heat immediately, avoiding boiling.
3. Create the Ganache: Pour the hot cream over the chopped milk chocolate. Add a pinch of salt and vanilla extract. Let it sit for a minute to melt the chocolate. Gently stir until the mixture becomes smooth and glossy.
4. Incorporate Butter: Add the softened butter and stir until fully incorporated. The ganache should be velvety and shiny.

5. Chill the Ganache: Cover the bowl with plastic wrap, ensuring it touches the surface of the ganache to prevent a skin from forming. Refrigerate the ganache for at least 2 hours, or until it firms up enough to handle.

6. Shape the Truffles: Once the ganache has chilled, use a spoon or a melon baller to scoop out small portions. Roll them into bite-sized balls and place them on a tray lined with wax paper.

7. Coating: Roll the milk chocolate truffles in your preferred coating. Options include cocoa powder for a classic finish, powdered sugar for added sweetness, or colored sprinkles for a playful touch.

8. Chill Again: Return the truffles to the refrigerator for about 30 minutes to set.

9. Serve and Enjoy: Your creamy milk chocolate truffles are now ready to be savored. Store them in an airtight container in the refrigerator for up to two weeks, though they are likely to disappear quickly!

Customizing Milk Chocolate Truffles

Milk chocolate truffles provide an excellent canvas for creativity. Here are some ways to customize them:

Fruit Infusion: Enhance the milk chocolate ganache with fruit purees like banana, strawberry, or apricot for a fruity twist.

Nuts and Caramel: Mix in finely chopped nuts (such as pecans or macadamias) or swirl in caramel for added texture and sweetness.

Spice It Up: Experiment with spices like cinnamon, nutmeg, or chai for a warm and aromatic flavor.

Citrus Zest: Add zest from citrus fruits like orange, lemon, or lime to brighten up the flavor.

Decorative Ideas

Elevate the presentation of your milk chocolate truffles with these decorative ideas:

Edible Gold or Silver Leaf: For an elegant touch, apply edible gold or silver leaf to the truffles before or after coating.

Drizzled Chocolate: Melt contrasting chocolate (white or dark) and drizzle it over the truffles for a visually appealing design.

Sprinkle Variations: Experiment with different types of colored sprinkles, edible glitter, or even crushed candies to add a burst of color and texture.

Dusting Patterns: Use stencils or templates to create intricate patterns with cocoa powder or powdered sugar on the truffle's surface.

Milk chocolate truffles offer a delightful contrast to dark chocolate truffles, and their creamy texture and versatility make them a crowd-pleaser.

Chapter 5: White Chocolate Elegance

White chocolate truffles embody sophistication and elegance with their creamy texture and sweet, vanilla-infused flavor. In this chapter, we'll guide you through crafting silky white chocolate truffles, explore various ways to infuse them with delightful flavors, and provide creative decoration ideas to elevate their elegance.

Recipe: Silky White Chocolate Truffles

Ingredients:

- 8 ounces (227 grams) high-quality white chocolate, finely chopped
- 1/2 cup (120 ml) heavy cream
- 2 tablespoons unsalted butter, softened
- 1/2 teaspoon pure vanilla extract
- Pinch of salt
- Coating of your choice (white chocolate shavings, edible flowers, or colored sugar)

Instructions:

1. Prepare the White Chocolate: Place the finely chopped white chocolate in a heatproof bowl.
2. Heat the Cream: In a saucepan over medium heat, warm the heavy cream until it begins to simmer. Remove it from the heat immediately, avoiding boiling.
3. Create the Ganache: Pour the hot cream over the chopped white chocolate. Add a pinch of salt and the vanilla extract. Allow it to sit for a minute to melt the chocolate. Gently stir until the mixture becomes smooth and glossy.
4. Incorporate Butter: Add the softened butter and stir until fully incorporated. The ganache should be creamy and shiny.

5. Chill the Ganache: Cover the bowl with plastic wrap, ensuring it touches the surface of the ganache to prevent a skin from forming. Refrigerate the ganache for at least 2 hours, or until it firms up enough to handle.

6. Shape the Truffles: Once the ganache has chilled, use a spoon or a melon baller to scoop out small portions. Roll them into bite-sized balls and place them on a tray lined with wax paper.

7. Coating: Roll the white chocolate truffles in your chosen coating. Options include white chocolate shavings for a luxurious look, edible flowers for an elegant touch, or colored sugar for a pop of color.

8. Chill Again: Return the truffles to the refrigerator for about 30 minutes to set.

9. Serve and Enjoy: Your silky white chocolate truffles are now ready to be savored. Store them in an airtight container in the refrigerator for up to two weeks, although they are sure to disappear quickly!

Flavoring White Chocolate Truffles

White chocolate truffles provide an excellent canvas for experimenting with various flavors:

Citrus Zest: Add zest from citrus fruits like lemon, lime, or orange to infuse a refreshing, zesty flavor.

Fruit Purees: Incorporate fruit purees such as mango, passion fruit, or pineapple for a tropical twist.

Herbal Infusions: Steep herbs like lavender, rosemary, or basil in the cream to impart subtle herbal notes.

Extracts and Liqueurs: Explore a wide range of extracts (e.g., almond, coconut) or liqueurs (e.g., limoncello, Chambord) to create unique flavor profiles.

Creative Decorations

Elevate the presentation of your white chocolate truffles with these creative decoration ideas:

White Chocolate Drizzle: Melt white chocolate and drizzle it over the truffles for an elegant and artistic touch.

Edible Flowers: Gently press edible flowers onto the truffles, creating a stunning visual effect.

Colored Sugar Crystals: Roll the truffles in colored sugar crystals to add a touch of sparkle and color.

Gold or Silver Dust: Use edible gold or silver dust to create a luxurious shimmer on the truffles.

White chocolate truffles exude elegance and can be customized with various flavors and decorative elements to suit any occasion.

Chapter 6: Vegan and Dairy-Free Variations

Indulgence knows no boundaries, and that includes catering to a vegan and dairy-free audience. In this chapter, we'll guide you through crafting delectable vegan chocolate truffles that are dairy-free and cruelty-free. We'll explore a recipe for vegan chocolate truffles, discuss dairy-free chocolate options, and provide suggestions for vegan coatings and decorations.

Recipe: Vegan Chocolate Truffles
Ingredients:

- 8 ounces (227 grams) dairy-free dark chocolate, finely chopped (look for vegan chocolate options)
- 1/2 cup (120 ml) full-fat coconut milk
- 2 tablespoons coconut oil, melted
- 1 teaspoon pure vanilla extract
- Pinch of salt
- Vegan coating of your choice (cocoa powder, shredded coconut, or crushed nuts)

Instructions:

1. Prepare the Dairy-Free Chocolate: Place the finely chopped dairy-free dark chocolate in a heatproof bowl.
2. Heat the Coconut Milk: In a saucepan over medium heat, warm the full-fat coconut milk until it begins to simmer. Remove it from the heat immediately; do not let it boil.
3. Create the Ganache: Pour the hot coconut milk over the chopped dairy-free chocolate. Add a pinch of salt and the vanilla extract. Allow it to sit for a minute to melt the chocolate. Gently stir until the mixture becomes smooth and glossy.

4. Incorporate Coconut Oil: Add the melted coconut oil and stir until fully incorporated. The ganache should be creamy and shiny.

5. Chill the Ganache: Cover the bowl with plastic wrap, ensuring it touches the surface of the ganache to prevent a skin from forming. Refrigerate the ganache for at least 2 hours, or until it firms up enough to handle.

6. Shape the Truffles: Once the ganache has chilled, use a spoon or a melon baller to scoop out small portions. Roll them into bite-sized balls and place them on a tray lined with wax paper.

7. Coating: Roll the vegan chocolate truffles in your preferred vegan coating. Options include cocoa powder for a classic finish, shredded coconut for a tropical touch, or crushed nuts for added texture.

8. Chill Again: Return the truffles to the refrigerator for about 30 minutes to set.

9. Serve and Enjoy: Your vegan chocolate truffles are now ready to be savored. Store them in an airtight container in the refrigerator for up to two weeks, although they are likely to disappear quickly!

Dairy-Free Chocolate Options

Selecting the right dairy-free chocolate is crucial for achieving the best flavor and texture in your vegan truffles. Look for these dairy-free chocolate options:

Dark Chocolate: Many dark chocolates are naturally dairy-free, but always check the label to ensure there are no milk solids or dairy-derived ingredients.

Vegan Chocolate Brands: Some brands specialize in vegan chocolates, specifically formulated without dairy. These chocolates are widely available and come in various cocoa percentages.

Cacao Butter: For a more customized approach, you can use cacao butter and cacao powder to create your dairy-free chocolate base. This gives you full control over the ingredients and sweetness level.

Vegan Coating and Decorations

Enhance the appeal of your vegan chocolate truffles with these vegan coating and decoration ideas:

Vegan Cocoa Powder: Use vegan-friendly cocoa powder to roll the truffles for that classic look.

Shredded Coconut: Shredded coconut is a great vegan coating option, adding a tropical flair to your truffles.

Crushed Nuts: Crushed nuts like almonds, cashews, or pistachios can provide a delightful nutty crunch and visual appeal.

Vegan Sprinkles: Look for vegan-friendly sprinkles made from natural colors and ingredients to add a pop of color and texture.

Edible Flowers: Edible flowers can create a visually stunning and sophisticated presentation for your vegan truffles.

Vegan and dairy-free chocolate truffles open up a world of possibilities, ensuring that everyone can enjoy these delightful treats.

Chapter 7: Nutty Infusions: Almond, Hazelnut, and More

Nuts and chocolate are a match made in heaven. In this chapter, we'll explore the art of infusing nutty flavors into your chocolate truffles. We'll provide a recipe for nutty chocolate truffles, delve into various nut flavors, and discuss nut coatings and garnishes to create the perfect nutty indulgence.

Recipe: Nutty Chocolate Truffles
Ingredients:

- 8 ounces (227 grams) high-quality dark or milk chocolate, finely chopped
- 1/2 cup (120 ml) heavy cream
- 2 tablespoons unsalted butter, softened
- 1/2 teaspoon pure vanilla extract
- Pinch of salt
- 1/2 cup finely chopped nuts of your choice (e.g., almonds, hazelnuts, pecans, walnuts)

Instructions:

1. Prepare the Chocolate: Place the finely chopped chocolate in a heatproof bowl.
2. Heat the Cream: In a saucepan over medium heat, warm the heavy cream until it begins to simmer. Remove it from the heat immediately; do not let it boil.
3. Create the Ganache: Pour the hot cream over the chopped chocolate. Add a pinch of salt and the vanilla extract. Allow it to sit for a minute to melt the chocolate. Gently stir until the mixture becomes smooth and glossy.
4. Incorporate Butter: Add the softened butter and stir until fully

incorporated. The ganache should be creamy and shiny.

5. Nut Infusion: Mix in the finely chopped nuts of your choice. This will infuse the ganache with delightful nutty flavors and provide a pleasing texture.

6. Chill the Ganache: Cover the bowl with plastic wrap, ensuring it touches the surface of the ganache to prevent a skin from forming. Refrigerate the ganache for at least 2 hours, or until it firms up enough to handle.

7. Shape the Truffles: Once the ganache has chilled, use a spoon or a melon baller to scoop out small portions. Roll them into bite-sized balls and place them on a tray lined with wax paper.

8. Coating: Roll the nutty chocolate truffles in your preferred coating, such as finely chopped nuts of the same type used in the ganache, for added texture and flavor.

9. Chill Again: Return the truffles to the refrigerator for about 30 minutes to set.

10. Serve and Enjoy: Your nutty chocolate truffles are now ready to be savored. Store them in an airtight container in the refrigerator for up to two weeks, though they are likely to be devoured much sooner!

Exploring Nut Flavors

Nuts offer a delightful range of flavors that can be infused into your chocolate truffles. Here are some nut options to consider:

Almonds: Almonds provide a subtle, sweet nuttiness and a satisfying crunch. You can use whole almonds or finely chop them for a more integrated flavor.

Hazelnuts: Hazelnuts impart a rich and buttery taste with hints of earthiness. They pair wonderfully with chocolate.

Pecans: Pecans add a distinctive sweetness and a buttery texture to your truffles, reminiscent of pecan pie.

Walnuts: Walnuts have a mild nutty flavor and work well with both dark and milk chocolate.

Nut Coatings and Garnishes

In addition to infusing nut flavors within the truffles, you can use nuts as coatings and garnishes:

Finely Chopped Nuts: Roll your truffles in finely chopped nuts of the same variety used in the ganache to create a delightful nutty crust.

Whole Nut Garnish: Place a single whole nut on top of each truffle for a visually appealing and nutty finish.

Toasted Nuts: Toasting nuts before using them as coatings or garnishes can enhance their flavor and aroma.

Candied Nuts: Consider using candied nuts for a sweet and crunchy contrast with the truffle's richness.

Nutty chocolate truffles offer a harmonious combination of creamy chocolate and nutty goodness.

Chapter 8: Fruity Flavors: Raspberry, Orange, and Beyond

The combination of chocolate and fruit is a classic and delightful pairing. In this chapter, we'll explore the world of fruity chocolate truffles, providing you with a recipe for fruity chocolate truffles, explaining how to infuse fresh and dried fruits into your creations, and suggesting fruit-infused coating ideas to make your truffles burst with vibrant flavors.

Recipe: Fruity Chocolate Truffles

Ingredients:

- 8 ounces (227 grams) high-quality dark or milk chocolate, finely chopped
- 1/2 cup (120 ml) heavy cream
- 2 tablespoons unsalted butter, softened
- 1/2 teaspoon pure vanilla extract
- Pinch of salt
- 1/4 cup fruit puree or finely chopped fresh fruit (e.g., raspberries, oranges, strawberries)
- Coating of your choice (cocoa powder, powdered sugar, or fruit-infused sugar)

Instructions:

1. Prepare the Chocolate: Place the finely chopped chocolate in a heatproof bowl.
2. Heat the Cream: In a saucepan over medium heat, warm the heavy cream until it begins to simmer. Remove it from the heat immediately; do not let it boil.
3. Create the Ganache: Pour the hot cream over the chopped chocolate. Add a pinch of salt and the vanilla extract. Allow it

to sit for a minute to melt the chocolate. Gently stir until the mixture becomes smooth and glossy.

4. Incorporate Butter: Add the softened butter and stir until fully incorporated. The ganache should be creamy and shiny.

5. Fruit Infusion: Mix in the fruit puree or finely chopped fresh fruit of your choice. This infusion will lend vibrant fruity flavors to your truffles.

6. Chill the Ganache: Cover the bowl with plastic wrap, ensuring it touches the surface of the ganache to prevent a skin from forming. Refrigerate the ganache for at least 2 hours, or until it firms up enough to handle.

7. Shape the Truffles: Once the ganache has chilled, use a spoon or a melon baller to scoop out small portions. Roll them into bite-sized balls and place them on a tray lined with wax paper.

8. Coating: Roll the fruity chocolate truffles in your preferred coating. Options include cocoa powder for a classic finish, powdered sugar for added sweetness, or fruit-infused sugar for a burst of fruity flavor.

9. Chill Again: Return the truffles to the refrigerator for about 30 minutes to set.

10. Serve and Enjoy: Your fruity chocolate truffles are now ready to be savored. Store them in an airtight container in the refrigerator for up to two weeks, although they are sure to be devoured much sooner!

Fresh and Dried Fruit Infusions

Infusing your truffles with fresh or dried fruits adds a burst of natural sweetness and flavor. Here are some ideas for fruit infusions:

Raspberry Delight: Fresh or freeze-dried raspberries can infuse a vibrant tartness and a lovely pink hue into your truffles.

Orange Zest: Orange zest and a hint of orange juice can bring bright citrus notes to your creations.

Strawberry Bliss: Fresh strawberries, pureed and strained, can lend a sweet and fragrant strawberry essence.

Passion Fruit: Passion fruit puree adds a tropical flair with its unique sweet-tart flavor.

Fruit-Infused Coating Ideas

To complement the fruity flavors within your truffles, consider fruit-infused coatings:

Fruit-Infused Sugar: Blend together dried fruit (e.g., strawberries, mangoes) and granulated sugar to create a vibrant and fruity sugar coating.

Fruit Powder: Dehydrate fresh fruit and grind it into a fine powder to dust your truffles for an intense burst of fruitiness.

Zest and Citrus Sugar: Combine citrus zest (e.g., lemon, lime) with sugar to create a zesty and aromatic coating.

Candied Fruit Bits: Finely chop candied fruits like orange peel or ginger to roll your truffles for a sweet and chewy crunch.

Fruity chocolate truffles offer a refreshing and vibrant twist to the classic chocolate truffle experience.

Chapter 9: Boozy Truffle Treats

For the adults who appreciate a little indulgence, boozy chocolate truffles are the perfect treat. In this chapter, we'll guide you through crafting delectable boozy chocolate truffles, provide a recipe to get you started, explain how to select and use liquors to infuse your truffles with unique flavors, and offer alcohol-free alternatives for those who prefer a non-alcoholic twist.

Recipe: Boozy Chocolate Truffles

Ingredients:

- 8 ounces (227 grams) high-quality dark or milk chocolate, finely chopped
- 1/2 cup (120 ml) heavy cream
- 2 tablespoons unsalted butter, softened
- Pinch of salt
- 2-3 tablespoons of your choice of liquor (e.g., rum, whiskey, liqueur)
- Coating of your choice (cocoa powder, chocolate shavings, or crushed nuts)

Instructions:

1. Prepare the Chocolate: Place the finely chopped chocolate in a heatproof bowl.
2. Heat the Cream: In a saucepan over medium heat, warm the heavy cream until it begins to simmer. Remove it from the heat immediately; do not let it boil.
3. Create the Ganache: Pour the hot cream over the chopped chocolate. Add a pinch of salt. Allow it to sit for a minute to melt the chocolate. Gently stir until the mixture becomes smooth and glossy.

4. Incorporate Butter: Add the softened butter and stir until fully incorporated. The ganache should be creamy and shiny.

5. Boozy Infusion: Stir in 2-3 tablespoons of your chosen liquor. The type of liquor will impart unique flavors and a hint of warmth to your truffles.

6. Chill the Ganache: Cover the bowl with plastic wrap, ensuring it touches the surface of the ganache to prevent a skin from forming. Refrigerate the ganache for at least 2 hours, or until it firms up enough to handle.

7. Shape the Truffles: Once the ganache has chilled, use a spoon or a melon baller to scoop out small portions. Roll them into bite-sized balls and place them on a tray lined with wax paper.

8. Coating: Roll the boozy chocolate truffles in your preferred coating. Options include cocoa powder for a classic finish, chocolate shavings for an extra chocolatey touch, or crushed nuts for added texture.

9. Chill Again: Return the truffles to the refrigerator for about 30 minutes to set.

10. Serve and Enjoy: Your boozy chocolate truffles are now ready to be savored. Store them in an airtight container in the refrigerator for up to two weeks, although they are likely to disappear much sooner!

Selecting and Using Liquors

Selecting the right liquor for your truffles is essential for achieving the desired flavor profile. Here are some popular options and their flavor characteristics:

Rum: Adds a sweet and slightly spicy flavor, often associated with tropical notes.

Whiskey: Imparts a warm and smoky essence, perfect for those who enjoy a hint of sophistication.

Liqueurs: Options like Grand Marnier, Amaretto, or Baileys offer a wide range of flavors, from citrusy and almond to creamy and rich.

Brandy: Provides a fruity and robust flavor, often with hints of cherry or apricot.

Kahlúa: Offers a coffee-infused and slightly sweet flavor, ideal for coffee lovers.

Alcohol-Free Alternatives

For those who prefer to enjoy their truffles without alcohol, you can achieve similar flavors with alcohol-free alternatives:

Extracts: Use alcohol-free extracts such as vanilla, almond, or coffee to infuse your truffles with flavor.

Fruit Juices: Substituting fruit juices like orange, cherry, or raspberry can provide fruity flavors without alcohol.

Coffee or Tea: Brew strong coffee or tea and use it to flavor your ganache for a non-alcoholic alternative.

Boozy chocolate truffles are a delightful way to enjoy the rich flavors of chocolate paired with the unique character of your favorite liquor.

Chapter 10: Coffee and Mocha Infused Truffles

For the coffee enthusiasts and mocha lovers, these coffee-infused truffles are a dream come true. In this chapter, we'll explore the world of coffee and mocha-infused truffles, providing you with a recipe for coffee lover's truffles, explaining how to infuse espresso and coffee flavors, and offering ideas for creating mocha swirl truffles that are sure to satisfy your caffeine cravings.

Recipe: Coffee Lover's Truffles

Ingredients:

- 8 ounces (227 grams) high-quality dark chocolate, finely chopped
- 1/2 cup (120 ml) heavy cream
- 2 tablespoons unsalted butter, softened
- Pinch of salt
- 2-3 tablespoons espresso or strong brewed coffee
- Coating of your choice (cocoa powder, chocolate-covered espresso beans, or coffee-infused sugar)

Instructions:

1. Prepare the Chocolate: Place the finely chopped chocolate in a heatproof bowl.
2. Heat the Cream: In a saucepan over medium heat, warm the heavy cream until it begins to simmer. Remove it from the heat immediately; do not let it boil.
3. Create the Ganache: Pour the hot cream over the chopped chocolate. Add a pinch of salt. Allow it to sit for a minute to melt the chocolate. Gently stir until the mixture becomes smooth and glossy.

4. Incorporate Butter: Add the softened butter and stir until fully incorporated. The ganache should be creamy and shiny.

5. Coffee Infusion: Stir in 2-3 tablespoons of espresso or strong brewed coffee. This infusion will infuse your truffles with rich coffee flavor and aroma.

6. Chill the Ganache: Cover the bowl with plastic wrap, ensuring it touches the surface of the ganache to prevent a skin from forming. Refrigerate the ganache for at least 2 hours, or until it firms up enough to handle.

7. Shape the Truffles: Once the ganache has chilled, use a spoon or a melon baller to scoop out small portions. Roll them into bite-sized balls and place them on a tray lined with wax paper.

8. Coating: Roll the coffee lover's truffles in your preferred coating. Options include cocoa powder for a classic coffee finish, chocolate-covered espresso beans for an extra caffeine kick, or coffee-infused sugar for a burst of coffee flavor.

9. Chill Again: Return the truffles to the refrigerator for about 30 minutes to set.

10. Serve and Enjoy: Your coffee lover's truffles are now ready to be savored. Store them in an airtight container in the refrigerator for up to two weeks, though they are likely to be enjoyed much sooner!

Espresso and Coffee Flavoring

Infusing your truffles with the essence of coffee is all about using the right coffee elements. Here's how to flavor your truffles:

Espresso: Adding espresso or strong brewed coffee to the ganache provides a robust and intense coffee flavor.

Coffee Extract: Coffee extract is a concentrated coffee flavoring that can be used in small amounts to impart a deep coffee taste.

Instant Coffee: Dissolve instant coffee granules in a small amount of hot water and use the resulting coffee solution to flavor your ganache.

Mocha Swirl Truffle Ideas

To create mocha swirl truffles, you can combine coffee and chocolate flavors in various ways:

Mocha Swirl: Prepare two separate ganaches, one with coffee infusion and one with plain chocolate. Roll small portions of each ganache together to create a marbled effect before shaping into truffles.

Coffee-Infused Layer: Create a layer of coffee-infused ganache and encase it within a layer of chocolate ganache. Roll in cocoa powder or chocolate shavings for added visual appeal.

Chocolate-Covered Espresso Bean Center: Insert a chocolate-covered espresso bean into the center of each truffle for a surprise burst of coffee flavor.

Coffee and mocha-infused truffles offer a delightful combination of rich chocolate and bold coffee flavors.

Chapter 11: Spices and Herbs: Unique Flavor Combinations

Exploring the realm of spices and herbs in your truffles can lead to unique and exciting flavor combinations. In this chapter, we'll delve into the art of spiced chocolate truffles, providing you with a recipe to get you started, suggesting spice and herb pairings, and offering ideas for aromatic spice coatings to elevate your truffle creations.

Recipe: Spiced Chocolate Truffles

Ingredients:

- 8 ounces (227 grams) high-quality dark or milk chocolate, finely chopped
- 1/2 cup (120 ml) heavy cream
- 2 tablespoons unsalted butter, softened
- Pinch of salt
- 1-2 teaspoons of your chosen spice or herb (e.g., cinnamon, cardamom, lavender, or chili powder)
- Coating of your choice (spice-infused sugar, cocoa powder, or finely chopped nuts)

Instructions:

1. Prepare the Chocolate: Place the finely chopped chocolate in a heatproof bowl.
2. Heat the Cream: In a saucepan over medium heat, warm the heavy cream until it begins to simmer. Remove it from the heat immediately; do not let it boil.
3. Create the Ganache: Pour the hot cream over the chopped chocolate. Add a pinch of salt. Allow it to sit for a minute to melt the chocolate. Gently stir until the mixture becomes smooth and glossy.

4. Incorporate Butter: Add the softened butter and stir until fully incorporated. The ganache should be creamy and shiny.

5. Spice or Herb Infusion: Stir in 1-2 teaspoons of your chosen spice or herb. This will infuse your truffles with unique and aromatic flavors.

6. Chill the Ganache: Cover the bowl with plastic wrap, ensuring it touches the surface of the ganache to prevent a skin from forming. Refrigerate the ganache for at least 2 hours, or until it firms up enough to handle.

7. Shape the Truffles: Once the ganache has chilled, use a spoon or a melon baller to scoop out small portions. Roll them into bite-sized balls and place them on a tray lined with wax paper.

8. Coating: Roll the spiced chocolate truffles in your preferred coating. Options include spice-infused sugar for a burst of spice flavor, cocoa powder for a classic finish, or finely chopped nuts for added texture.

9. Chill Again: Return the truffles to the refrigerator for about 30 minutes to set.

10. Serve and Enjoy: Your spiced chocolate truffles are now ready to be savored. Store them in an airtight container in the refrigerator for up to two weeks, though they are likely to disappear much sooner!

Spice and Herb Pairings

Pairing spices and herbs with chocolate opens up a world of exciting flavor combinations. Here are some ideas to get you started:

Cinnamon: Adds a warm and comforting spice that pairs exceptionally well with dark chocolate.

Cardamom: Imparts a unique and exotic floral note that complements both dark and milk chocolate.

Lavender: Offers a floral and aromatic touch that elevates the elegance of your truffles.

Chili Powder: Provides a subtle heat that beautifully contrasts with the sweetness of chocolate.

Rosemary: Adds an earthy and herbaceous aroma that can be surprisingly delightful with chocolate.

Aromatic Spice Coatings

To enhance the aromatic experience of your spiced truffles, consider using aromatic spice coatings:

Spice-Infused Sugar: Combine your chosen spice with granulated sugar and use it to roll your truffles for an intense burst of spice flavor.

Spice Dust: Grind spices into a fine powder and dust your truffles for an aromatic and visually appealing finish.

Herb Garnish: Top your truffles with small herb leaves, such as rosemary or lavender, for an elegant touch.

Chili Chocolate: Incorporate chili powder into the ganache and dust your truffles with a blend of cocoa powder and chili powder for a spicy kick.

Spiced chocolate truffles offer a captivating fusion of flavors and aromas that will surprise and delight your taste buds.

Chapter 12: Healthier Options: Avocado and Coconut Truffles

For those looking for a guilt-free chocolate treat, these avocado and coconut truffles are the perfect solution. In this chapter, we'll explore the world of healthier chocolate truffles, providing you with a recipe for guilt-free chocolate truffles, explaining how to use avocado for creaminess, and showcasing the use of coconut and healthy sweeteners to create treats that are as wholesome as they are delicious.

Recipe: Guilt-Free Chocolate Truffles
Ingredients:

- 8 ounces (227 grams) high-quality dark chocolate, finely chopped
- 1 ripe avocado, peeled and pitted
- 2 tablespoons unsweetened cocoa powder
- 2 tablespoons honey or maple syrup (adjust to taste)
- 1 teaspoon pure vanilla extract
- Pinch of salt
- Unsweetened shredded coconut, for coating

Instructions:

Melt the Chocolate: Place the finely chopped dark chocolate in a heatproof bowl. Melt it using a microwave in 20-second intervals or over a double boiler until smooth. Allow it to cool slightly.

Blend the Avocado: In a food processor or blender, combine the ripe avocado, unsweetened cocoa powder, honey or maple syrup, pure vanilla extract, and a pinch of salt. Blend until you have a smooth and creamy avocado mixture.

Combine Chocolate and Avocado: Pour the melted chocolate into the avocado mixture. Blend until everything is fully combined, creating a rich and creamy chocolate mixture.

Chill the Mixture: Cover the bowl and refrigerate the mixture for at least 1 hour, or until it firms up enough to handle.

Shape the Truffles: Once the mixture has chilled, use a spoon or a melon baller to scoop out small portions. Roll them into bite-sized balls and place them on a tray lined with wax paper.

Coat with Coconut: Roll the avocado and chocolate truffles in unsweetened shredded coconut, pressing gently to adhere.

Chill Again: Return the truffles to the refrigerator for about 30 minutes to set.

Serve and Enjoy: Your guilt-free chocolate truffles are now ready to be savored. Store them in an airtight container in the refrigerator for up to one week.

Using Avocado for Creaminess

Avocado is a fantastic natural substitute for cream in chocolate truffles. Its creamy texture and mild flavor blend seamlessly with chocolate, creating a luscious ganache without the need for heavy cream or dairy.

Coconut and Healthy Sweeteners

In this healthier truffle recipe, we incorporate coconut and healthy sweeteners:

Coconut: Unsweetened shredded coconut is used as both a coating and an ingredient in the avocado mixture. It adds a delightful tropical flavor and texture.

Healthy Sweeteners: Instead of refined sugar, this recipe calls for natural sweeteners like honey or maple syrup. You can adjust the sweetness to your liking.

These healthier options offer a delicious way to enjoy chocolate truffles while keeping an eye on your health-conscious choices.

Chapter 13: Kid-Friendly Truffle Creations

Truffles aren't just for adults; they can be a delightful treat for kids too! In this chapter, we'll dive into the world of kid-friendly truffle creations, providing you with a recipe for fun and colorful truffles, suggesting kid-approved flavors, and offering ideas for kid-friendly decorations that will make truffle-making an enjoyable family activity.

Recipe: Fun and Colorful Truffles

Ingredients:

- 8 ounces (227 grams) high-quality white chocolate, finely chopped
- 1/4 cup (60 ml) heavy cream
- 2 tablespoons unsalted butter, softened
- Pinch of salt
- 1/2 teaspoon pure vanilla extract
- Food coloring (gel or liquid) in various colors
- Sprinkles, colored sugar, or edible glitter for decorating

Instructions:

Prepare the White Chocolate: Place the finely chopped white chocolate in a heatproof bowl.

Heat the Cream: In a saucepan over medium heat, warm the heavy cream until it begins to simmer. Remove it from the heat immediately; do not let it boil.

Create the Ganache: Pour the hot cream over the chopped white chocolate. Add a pinch of salt and the vanilla extract. Allow it to sit for a minute to melt the chocolate. Gently stir until the mixture becomes smooth and glossy.

Incorporate Butter: Add the softened butter and stir until fully incorporated. The ganache should be creamy and shiny.

Color the Ganache: Divide the ganache into separate bowls, one for each color you want to create. Add a few drops of food coloring to each bowl and mix until you achieve your desired color intensity.

Chill the Ganache: Cover each bowl with plastic wrap, ensuring it touches the surface of the ganache to prevent a skin from forming. Refrigerate the ganache for at least 2 hours, or until it firms up enough to handle.

Shape the Truffles: Once the ganache has chilled, use a spoon or a melon baller to scoop out small portions of each colored ganache. Roll them into bite-sized balls and place them on a tray lined with wax paper.

Decorate with Sprinkles: Roll the colorful truffles in your choice of sprinkles, colored sugar, or edible glitter to add a fun and whimsical touch.

Chill Again: Return the truffles to the refrigerator for about 30 minutes to set.

Serve and Enjoy: Your fun and colorful truffles are now ready to be enjoyed by kids of all ages. Store them in an airtight container in the refrigerator for up to one week.

Kid-Approved Flavors

Kids have a wide range of flavor preferences, and you can cater to their tastes with various flavors:

Vanilla: Classic and universally loved, vanilla-flavored truffles are always a hit.

Fruit: Incorporate fruit flavors like strawberry, raspberry, or banana for a fruity twist.

Cookies and Cream: Crushed cookies mixed with white chocolate ganache create a cookies-and-cream delight.

Peanut Butter: Peanut butter and chocolate are a winning combination for many kids.

Kid-Friendly Decorations

Make truffle-making even more enjoyable for kids with creative decorations:

Sprinkles: Colorful sprinkles add a playful and festive touch to truffles.

Colored Sugar: Use colored sugar to coat the truffles for a sparkly and sweet finish.

Edible Glitter: Edible glitter adds a magical and enchanting element to the truffles.

Mini Candies: Small candies like M&M's or mini chocolate chips can be pressed into the truffles for added texture and flavor.

Kid-friendly truffle creations offer a wonderful opportunity to get kids involved in the kitchen and spark their creativity.

Chapter 14: Truffle Shapes and Decorations

Elevate your truffle-making skills by mastering the art of truffle shapes and decorations. In this chapter, we'll explore various shaping techniques, offer creative ideas for decorating with chocolate and edible elements, and provide tips for achieving professional-looking truffles that are as stunning as they are delicious.

Shaping Techniques

Creating visually appealing truffle shapes can make your treats even more enticing. Here are some shaping techniques to explore:

Classic Spheres: The most common truffle shape is a simple sphere. Roll the ganache into small balls for a timeless presentation.

Rounded Cones: For a variation on the classic sphere, shape the ganache into small cones by gently tapering one end. It adds an elegant touch.

Rectangles: Flatten the ganache and cut it into small rectangles or squares for a modern and minimalist appearance.

Ovals: Roll the ganache into oval shapes for a sleek and elongated truffle presentation.

Freeform: Embrace creativity by shaping your truffles into unique freeform designs that reflect your personal style.

Decorating with Chocolate and Edible Elements

Decorating your truffles is an opportunity to showcase your artistic flair. Here are some creative ideas:

Dipped Truffles: Dip your truffles in melted chocolate (dark, milk, or white) to create a smooth and glossy coating. Drizzle contrasting chocolate on top for an eye-catching finish.

Chocolate Shavings: Use a vegetable peeler to create delicate chocolate shavings or curls. Gently press them onto the truffles for a beautiful texture.

Edible Gold and Silver Leaf: Add a touch of luxury by applying edible gold or silver leaf to your truffles. They create a stunning metallic finish.

Sprinkles and Nonpareils: Sprinkle colorful nonpareils or a variety of sprinkles onto the dipped truffles for a fun and festive appearance.

Crushed Nuts: Roll your truffles in finely chopped nuts (e.g., almonds, hazelnuts) to add a delightful crunch and a rustic look.

Cocoa Powder: A classic choice, rolling truffles in cocoa powder creates an elegant matte finish.

Colored Cocoa Butter: Paint truffles with colored cocoa butter for a vibrant and artistic design.

Edible Flowers: Garnish your truffles with edible flowers like pansies or violets for a natural and delicate touch.

Tips for Professional-Looking Truffles

Achieving professional-looking truffles requires attention to detail. Here are some tips to help you master the art:

Consistent Size: Aim for uniformity in size when shaping your truffles. This makes for a visually appealing presentation.

Smooth Coatings: When dipping truffles in chocolate, ensure the coating is smooth and free of streaks. Use a fork or dipping tool for precision.

Chilled Ganache: Keep the ganache cold while working with it to make shaping and handling easier.

Even Coatings: If you're rolling truffles in coatings like cocoa powder or nuts, ensure an even distribution for a polished look.

Clean Edges: For cut truffles, use a sharp knife to create clean, sharp edges.

Piping Bags: When precision is crucial, consider using a piping bag to create beautifully shaped truffles.

Practice: Don't be discouraged if your first truffles aren't perfect. Like any art form, practice makes perfect.

Mastering truffle shapes and decorations allows you to transform your creations into edible works of art.

Chapter 15: Truffle Coating Techniques

Coating your truffles is an art that can take your creations to the next level. In this chapter, we'll delve into mastering the art of truffle coating, explore different coating options, and provide troubleshooting tips to help you overcome any coating issues you may encounter.

Mastering the Art of Coating

Coating truffles is not just about aesthetics; it also enhances the flavor and texture of your creations. To master the art of truffle coating, follow these essential steps:

Preparation: Ensure your truffles are chilled and firm before coating. A cold ganache is easier to work with and holds its shape.

Melted Chocolate: Use high-quality melted chocolate for dipping. Melt it gently, either in a microwave in short intervals or over a double boiler. Stir until smooth.

Dipping Tools: Invest in dipping tools or use a fork to submerge the truffles in the melted chocolate. This ensures a smooth, even coating.

Dip and Tap: Dip a truffle into the melted chocolate, allowing excess chocolate to drip off. Tap the truffle gently against the side of the bowl to remove any excess chocolate.

Set on Parchment: Place the coated truffle on a parchment paper-lined tray. This prevents sticking and allows the chocolate to set evenly.

Decorate: While the chocolate is still wet, add any decorations like sprinkles, nuts, or drizzled chocolate.

Chill: Once all the truffles are coated and decorated, chill them in the refrigerator to allow the chocolate to set completely.

Different Coating Options

The coating you choose can dramatically change the texture and flavor of your truffles. Here are some popular coating options to consider:

Cocoa Powder: A classic choice, cocoa powder adds a soft, matte finish and enhances the chocolate flavor.

Chocolate Shavings: Finely grated chocolate or chocolate shavings provide a luxurious and visually appealing coating.

Crushed Nuts: Chopped nuts (e.g., almonds, hazelnuts, or pistachios) add a delightful crunch and a nutty flavor.

Sprinkles: Colorful sprinkles or nonpareils are perfect for adding a festive and playful touch to your truffles.

Powdered Sugar: Dusting truffles with powdered sugar gives them an elegant and snowy appearance.

Coconut: Shredded coconut, toasted or untoasted, provides a tropical and slightly chewy coating.

Colored Candy Melts: Dip truffles in colored candy melts for a vibrant and visually striking appearance.

Edible Glitter: Edible glitter or dust adds a touch of sparkle and enchantment to your truffles.

Troubleshooting Coating Issues

Coating truffles can sometimes present challenges. Here are solutions to common coating issues:

Cracking Chocolate: If your chocolate coating cracks, it may have cooled too quickly. Ensure your truffles are at room temperature before dipping and avoid drastic temperature changes.

Streaky Coating: Uneven or streaky coatings can result from overheated chocolate. Melt the chocolate gently, and stir until smooth.

Dull Appearance: If your chocolate loses its shine, it may have cooled too slowly. Allow the chocolate to set at room temperature or in the refrigerator to regain its gloss.

Excess Coating: To avoid overly thick coatings, tap off excess chocolate after dipping. Ensure the coating is evenly distributed.

Decorations Won't Stick: Apply decorations like sprinkles or nuts while the chocolate is still wet to ensure they adhere properly.

Mastering truffle coating techniques is essential to creating visually stunning and delicious truffles.

Chapter 16: Tips for Perfectly Tempered Chocolate

Achieving perfectly tempered chocolate is crucial for creating beautiful and professional-looking truffles. In this chapter, we'll dive into understanding chocolate tempering, explore various tempering methods, and provide troubleshooting tips to help you conquer any tempering problems that may arise during your truffle-making journey.

Understanding Chocolate Tempering

Tempering chocolate is the process of heating and cooling chocolate to specific temperatures to ensure it sets properly, giving it a glossy appearance and a satisfying snap when bitten into. Properly tempered chocolate is essential for coating truffles because it prevents dullness, blooming (white streaks), and a soft, sticky texture.

The key temperatures for tempering dark chocolate are:

Melting: 115°F to 120°F (46°C to 49°C)

Cooling: 80°F to 85°F (27°C to 29°C)

Working: 88°F to 90°F (31°C to 32°C)

For milk chocolate and white chocolate, adjust the temperatures slightly lower.

Various Tempering Methods

There are several methods for tempering chocolate, each with its pros and cons. Here are a few common ones:

Seed Method: This method involves melting chocolate, adding small pieces of unmelted chocolate (seeds), and stirring until it cools to the desired working temperature. The seeds help "inoculate" the melted chocolate with the correct crystal structure.

Tabling Method: This traditional method requires pouring two-thirds of the melted chocolate onto a marble or granite surface and working it with a spatula until it cools to the desired working temperature. Then, it's combined with the remaining melted chocolate.

Microwave Method: Microwave the chocolate in short bursts, stirring between each burst, until it reaches the melting temperature. Then, cool it down with small, unmelted chocolate pieces until you reach the working temperature.

Seeding Method: This method involves adding small chocolate callets (chips) or chunks to the melted chocolate and stirring until they melt, bringing the chocolate to the desired working temperature.

Troubleshooting Tempering Problems

Even experienced chocolatiers encounter tempering issues from time to time. Here are some common problems and their solutions:

Chocolate is Too Thick: If the chocolate becomes too thick or difficult to work with, it may have cooled too much. Gently reheat it in short bursts until it reaches the working temperature again.

Chocolate is Too Thin: If the chocolate is too thin and runny, it may have been overheated. Allow it to cool slightly at room temperature, stirring occasionally until it thickens.

Bloom: If your truffles develop white streaks or spots (bloom) after setting, it's a sign of improper tempering. Re-temper the chocolate and recoat the truffles.

Grainy Texture: A grainy texture can result from improper tempering. Start over by melting the chocolate and re-tempering it.

Chocolate Won't Set: If your chocolate doesn't set properly, it may not have been tempered correctly. You may need to start over or re-temper the chocolate.

Tempering chocolate can be challenging, but with practice and patience, you can master this essential skill for creating exquisite truffles.

Chapter 17: Storing and Gifting Your Truffles

Creating delectable truffles is only half the journey; knowing how to store them properly and present them as delightful gifts completes the experience. In this chapter, we'll explore proper storage practices for keeping your truffles at their best, discuss gift packaging and presentation to impress your recipients, and offer homemade truffle gift ideas for every occasion.

Proper Storage Practices

To maintain the freshness and quality of your truffles, follow these proper storage practices:

Refrigeration: Truffles should be stored in an airtight container in the refrigerator. The cool temperature helps keep the chocolate from melting or becoming too soft.

Layering: Place a sheet of parchment paper between layers of truffles to prevent sticking and flavor transfer.

Avoid Odors: Store truffles away from strongly scented foods, as chocolate easily absorbs odors.

Consume Promptly: While truffles can last for several weeks when stored properly, they are best enjoyed within a week or two for optimal freshness.

Gift Packaging and Presentation

When gifting your truffles, presentation is key. Elevate your truffle-gifting game with these packaging and presentation ideas:

Elegant Boxes: Invest in decorative boxes specifically designed for chocolates. They come in various sizes and designs, making them perfect for presenting your truffles.

Tin Tie Bags: Small tin tie bags with clear windows allow your recipients to see the delicious truffles inside. They're perfect for a rustic or homemade touch.

Cellophane Wrapping: Wrap individual truffles in colorful cellophane or wax paper and tie them with a ribbon for a simple yet charming presentation.

DIY Gift Wrap: Create your own custom gift wrap by decorating plain boxes or bags with stickers, stamps, or hand-drawn designs.

Tied with Ribbon: Place truffles in a clear container or a simple box and tie the package with a luxurious ribbon. Add a personalized tag for an extra touch.

Decorative Tins: Consider using decorative tins or containers that can be reused after the truffles are enjoyed.

Gift Baskets: Combine truffles with other gourmet treats like coffee, tea, or wine in a gift basket for a lavish gift.

Homemade Truffle Gift Ideas

Looking to make your truffle gifts even more special? Here are some homemade truffle gift ideas for various occasions:

Weddings: Create personalized truffle favors for wedding guests by customizing the flavors and packaging to match the wedding theme.

Holidays: Craft holiday-themed truffles, such as pumpkin spice for Thanksgiving or peppermint for Christmas, and package them in festive containers.

Birthdays: Design a birthday gift box filled with an assortment of truffle flavors, each wrapped in colorful paper or decorated with birthday-themed toppings.

Anniversaries: Craft a romantic truffle assortment featuring flavors like champagne or strawberries and cream, packaged in an elegant box.

Thank You Gifts: Show appreciation with a thank-you gift that includes a selection of truffles and a heartfelt note.

New Baby: Celebrate the arrival of a new baby with truffles in pastel colors and baby-themed decorations.

Get Well Soon: Send a thoughtful get-well gift of truffles to brighten someone's day during recovery.

Just Because: Sometimes, the best gifts are the ones given for no reason at all. Surprise a friend or loved one with a truffle assortment to bring a smile to their face.

Remember that the thought and effort you put into the presentation of your truffle gifts can make them even more cherished by the recipients. Whether it's a special occasion or a simple gesture of appreciation, homemade truffles make wonderful gifts that are sure to be savored and remembered.

Chapter 18: Truffle Troubleshooting

Even experienced truffle makers can face challenges in the kitchen. In this chapter, we'll explore common truffle-making challenges, provide solutions and fixes to overcome them, and offer expert tips to ensure your truffle-making endeavors are a resounding success.

Common Truffle-Making Challenges

Ganache Too Soft: If your ganache is too soft to shape into truffles, it may not have cooled sufficiently. To fix this, refrigerate it until it firms up, then proceed with shaping.

Ganache Too Hard: Conversely, if your ganache becomes too hard to work with, it may have been chilled for too long. Let it sit at room temperature for a while to soften slightly.

Ganache Split: A split ganache, where the fat separates from the liquid, can occur due to overheating or adding too much cold liquid. To remedy this, gently reheat the ganache and whisk until it emulsifies.

Truffles Won't Hold Shape: If your truffles lose their shape or become misshapen when rolling, ensure your hands and tools are clean, and work quickly to prevent melting.

Chocolate Blooms: The appearance of white streaks on your truffles (chocolate bloom) is caused by temperature fluctuations. To fix this, re-temper and coat the truffles.

Inconsistent Flavor: If the flavor of your truffles isn't as pronounced as you'd like, adjust the ingredients and flavorings in your ganache mixture. Experiment until you achieve the desired taste.

Messy Coatings: Uneven or messy truffle coatings can result from improper dipping techniques. Dip the truffles carefully and tap off excess chocolate to create a clean finish.

Solutions and Fixes

Here are solutions and fixes to address common truffle-making challenges:

Overcome Soft Ganache: If your ganache is too soft to shape, refrigerate it until firm. You can also add a bit more melted chocolate to thicken it.

Fix Hard Ganache: If your ganache becomes too hard, allow it to sit at room temperature for a while to soften. If necessary, gently reheat it in short bursts in the microwave.

Emulsify Split Ganache: To rescue a split ganache, gently heat it and whisk until it comes back together. If it remains separated, try adding a small amount of hot cream and continue whisking.

Shape Misshapen Truffles: If truffles lose their shape, quickly reshape them using your hands or a truffle mold, and then chill them again.

Combat Chocolate Blooms: To eliminate chocolate bloom, re-temper the chocolate and re-coat the truffles, ensuring a proper temper this time.

Enhance Flavor: Adjust the flavor of your ganache by incorporating additional flavorings, extracts, or spices until it reaches the desired taste.

Improve Coating Technique: Practice dipping truffles until you master the technique, ensuring even and neat coatings.

Expert Tips for Success

To consistently create perfect truffles, consider these expert tips:

Precision Matters: Use a kitchen scale for accurate measurements, especially when dealing with chocolate, which is sensitive to ratios.

Quality Ingredients: Always choose high-quality chocolate and fresh ingredients for the best results.

Temperature Control: Pay close attention to temperatures throughout the truffle-making process, from ganache to coating.

Patience is Key: Be patient when tempering chocolate, as rushing the process can lead to tempering issues.

Practice Makes Perfect: Don't be discouraged by initial challenges. Truffle making is an art that improves with practice.

Experiment and Innovate: Feel free to experiment with flavors, coatings, and decorations to create unique truffle creations.

Enjoy the Process: Making truffles is a delightful culinary adventure. Embrace the journey and savor the delicious results.

Troubleshooting is a valuable skill in the world of truffle making. By understanding common issues, applying solutions, and incorporating expert tips, you can create delectable truffles that consistently impress and satisfy your taste buds.

Chapter 19: Chocolate Pairings and Tasting Notes

Enhance your truffle-making experience by exploring the world of chocolate pairings and tasting notes. In this chapter, we'll guide you through a chocolate tasting experience, helping you understand flavor profiles and descriptions to create harmonious and delicious truffle combinations.

Chocolate Tasting Experience

Before diving into chocolate pairings, it's essential to appreciate the nuances of chocolate through a tasting experience. Here's a step-by-step guide:

Selection: Choose a variety of high-quality chocolates to taste. Include dark, milk, and white chocolates with different cocoa percentages.

Preparation: Break each chocolate type into small pieces or segments, providing one piece for each participant.

Observation: Begin by observing the appearance of the chocolate. Note its color, sheen, and any texture or imperfections on the surface.

Aroma: Bring the chocolate close to your nose and inhale deeply. Pay attention to the aroma and try to identify any scents, such as fruit, vanilla, nuts, or spices.

Texture: Take a small bite and notice the texture. Is it smooth, creamy, or grainy? Does it melt quickly or linger on the palate?

Flavor Journey: As the chocolate melts in your mouth, focus on the flavor journey. Start with the initial taste, then note any changes in flavor as it develops. Is it sweet, bitter, fruity, or nutty?

Finish: Pay attention to the finish or aftertaste. Does the chocolate leave a pleasant, lingering flavor, or does it dissipate quickly?

Pairing Notes: Record your tasting notes for each chocolate type, including its aroma, flavor, texture, and overall impression.

Flavor Profiles and Descriptions

Understanding the flavor profiles of different chocolates is crucial for creating harmonious truffle pairings. Here are some common flavor profiles and descriptions for various types of chocolate:

Dark Chocolate (70% cocoa or higher):

Flavor: Intense cocoa flavor with notes of red fruit, dried fruit, and a touch of earthiness.

Aroma: Rich and complex, often with hints of coffee, tobacco, and dark berries.

Texture: Smooth and velvety, with a slow melt.

Pairing Ideas: Dark chocolate pairs well with bold flavors like coffee, nuts, spices, and citrus.

Milk Chocolate:

Flavor: Creamy and sweet with pronounced dairy notes, hints of caramel, and a subtle cocoa presence.

Aroma: Warm and inviting, reminiscent of cocoa and vanilla.

Texture: Soft and creamy, with a quick melt.

Pairing Ideas: Milk chocolate complements flavors like caramel, nuts, berries, and toffee.

White Chocolate:

Flavor: Rich and buttery with pronounced vanilla and dairy flavors and a sweetness akin to condensed milk.

Aroma: Sweet and inviting, reminiscent of vanilla and cream.

Texture: Silky and smooth, with a quick melt.

Pairing Ideas: White chocolate pairs beautifully with fruits like strawberries, passion fruit, and citrus, as well as floral and nutty flavors.

Ruby Chocolate:

Flavor: Fruity and slightly tart, with natural berry notes and a creamy undertone.

Aroma: Fresh and fruity, often reminiscent of raspberry or cherry.

Texture: Smooth and creamy, with a melt similar to milk chocolate.

Pairing Ideas: Ruby chocolate complements fruits like berries, citrus, and tropical fruits, as well as herbs and spices.

Flavored Chocolates:

Flavor: Varies depending on the added ingredients, such as spices, herbs, fruit extracts, or liquors.

Aroma: Reflects the specific flavors and aromatics incorporated.

Texture: Typically mirrors the base chocolate type.

Pairing Ideas: Experiment with complementary flavors based on the added ingredients.

Understanding the flavor profiles and descriptions of different chocolates allows you to create harmonious pairings with ingredients and flavors that enhance and complement the chocolate's characteristics.

Chapter 20: Beyond Truffles: Desserts and Treats

While truffles are delightful on their own, there are countless ways to incorporate these chocolate gems into other desserts and treats. In this chapter, we'll explore how to use truffles in various dessert creations, share truffle-inspired dessert recipes, and provide creative ways to enjoy chocolate truffles beyond the classic bite-sized form.

Using Truffles in Other Desserts

Truffles can be a versatile ingredient in your dessert repertoire. Here's how to use truffles in other dessert creations:

Ice Cream: Chop truffles into small pieces and fold them into your homemade ice cream for a luxurious and indulgent treat.

Brownies: Swirl melted truffles into brownie batter before baking to infuse your brownies with a rich chocolatey flavor.

Cake Fillings: Incorporate finely grated truffles into cake fillings or frostings for a decadent surprise.

Mousse: Add finely chopped truffles to your chocolate mousse recipe for extra texture and flavor.

Hot Chocolate: Stir a truffle into a steaming cup of hot chocolate for a creamy, chocolatey experience.

Tarts: Use truffle ganache as a filling for chocolate tarts or tartlets for a luscious dessert.

Truffle-Inspired Dessert Recipes

Here are some delicious truffle-inspired dessert recipes to try:

Truffle Cheesecake:

Create a classic cheesecake with a chocolate truffle twist by incorporating finely chopped truffles into the cream cheese filling. Top with ganache and whole truffles for an elegant presentation.

Truffle Fondue:

Make a decadent chocolate fondue by melting truffles with cream. Serve with a variety of dippable treats like fruits, marshmallows, and cookies for a memorable dessert experience.

Truffle Tiramisu:

Layer truffle-infused ladyfingers with mascarpone cheese and a dusting of cocoa powder for a luxurious take on the classic Italian dessert.

Truffle Stuffed Crepes:

Fill delicate crepes with a truffle ganache and top with fresh berries and a drizzle of chocolate sauce for an exquisite brunch or dessert option.

Truffle Brownie Sundae:

Create the ultimate brownie sundae by serving warm truffle-infused brownies topped with vanilla ice cream, chocolate sauce, and chopped nuts.

Truffle Panna Cotta:

Incorporate melted truffles into a creamy panna cotta base for a silky dessert. Garnish with raspberry coulis and fresh berries.

Creative Ways to Enjoy Chocolate Truffles

Don't limit your enjoyment of chocolate truffles to traditional eating. Get creative with these alternative ways to savor truffles:

Truffle-Infused Coffee: Drop a truffle into your freshly brewed coffee and let it melt for a delightful mocha-like experience.

Truffle Hot Cocoa Spoons: Make truffle-infused hot cocoa spoons by dipping truffles in melted chocolate and allowing them to harden on spoons. Stir them into hot milk for a luxurious hot chocolate.

Truffle Garnish: Grate truffles over other desserts like cakes, pies, or even a bowl of fresh fruit to add an elegant finishing touch.

Truffle Fondant: Create truffle fondant by blending truffles with powdered sugar and rolling the mixture into bite-sized balls for a sweet treat.

Truffle Milkshake: Blend truffles into a milkshake for a rich and creamy indulgence.

Truffle Topping: Crumble truffles over vanilla ice cream, yogurt, or pancakes as a delectable topping.

Using truffles in other desserts and treats allows you to explore new dimensions of flavor and creativity. The rich, decadent nature of truffles can transform ordinary desserts into extraordinary culinary experiences. Whether you're experimenting with truffle-infused recipes or savoring them in inventive ways, the possibilities are endless for enjoying these chocolate delights.

Congratulations on completing your culinary journey through the "Chocolate Truffle Cookbook"! We've explored the art of truffle making from start to finish, covering essential techniques, a variety of mouthwatering recipes, and creative ways to enjoy chocolate truffles.

Throughout this cookbook, you've learned to master the craft of creating silky ganache, tempering chocolate to perfection, shaping and coating truffles with finesse, and troubleshooting common challenges. You've also discovered a world of flavor possibilities, from classic dark chocolate truffles to unique variations like fruity, nutty, boozy, and even vegan options.

But our journey didn't stop at truffles alone. We delved into the art of presentation and gifting, ensuring your truffles are not only delicious but also beautifully presented. You've explored the magic of chocolate pairings and tasting notes, allowing you to create harmonious combinations that elevate your truffles to new heights.

And finally, we ventured beyond truffles, uncovering exciting ways to use truffles in other desserts and treats, from cheesecakes to fondue to hot cocoa spoons.

Remember that making chocolate truffles is not just about creating a sweet treat; it's a form of culinary artistry that allows you to express your creativity and share delicious moments with loved ones. Whether you're crafting truffles for special occasions, gifting them as tokens of appreciation, or simply indulging in a personal treat, the joy of truffle making is in both the process and the result.

We hope this cookbook has ignited your passion for crafting chocolate truffles and inspired you to explore the endless possibilities within the world of chocolate and confectionery. Continue to experiment, create, and share the love of truffles with those around you.

Thank you for joining us on this delicious journey. May your truffle-making adventures be filled with sweet success and delectable moments. Enjoy every bite!